21st Century Skills INNOVATION LIBRARY

Contents

Chapter 1

What Does It Mean to Hack Fashion?

Your clothing says a lot about who you are. Wearing the same clothes as other people can tell the world you are part of a group. A local baseball jersey might mean you're on the team. A major league jersey means you're probably a fan. Choir robes, school uniforms, and bowling shirts all identify wearers as part of a group.

Sometimes people like to follow fads with clothes that are just a little different from what others are wearing. For example, people wear sneakers, but there are many styles and colors to choose from. A lot of people wear rubber band bracelets, but they're all a bit different. These choices allow people to show their individuality while following style trends.

But have you ever wished you had clothing unlike anything other people are wearing? If so, maybe you're meant to be a fashion hacker. Many people think of hacking as breaking into other people's computers. However, hacking is about more than just computers. Hackers modify items to improve them or

Century Skills INNOVATION LIBRARY

MAKERS
As Innovators

Hacking Fashion:
T-Shirts

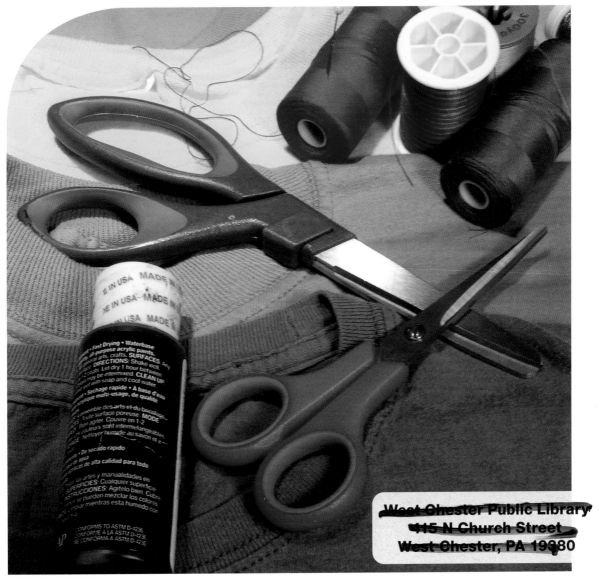

CHERRY LAKE PUBLISHING • ANN ARBOR, MICHIGAN

by Kristin Fontichiaro

CHERRY
LAKE
Publishing

A Note to Adults: Please review the instructions for the activities in this book before allowing children to do them. Be sure to help them with any activities you do not think they can safely complete on their own.

A Note to Kids: Be sure to ask an adult for help with th... activities when you need it. Always put your safety first!

Published in the United States of America by Cherry Lake Publishing
Ann Arbor, Michigan
www.cherrylakepublishing.com

Series editor: Kristin Fontichiaro

Photo Credits: Cover and pages 1, 5, 7, 9, 11, 13, 14, 18, 19, 21, and 28, courtesy of Michigan Makers; pages 24, 25, 27, courtesy of Kristin Fontichiaro.

Library of Congress Cataloging-in-Publication Data
Fontichiaro, Kristin, author.
  Hacking fashion t-shirts / by Kristin Fontichiaro.
      pages cm. — (21st century skills innovation library. Makers as innovators)
  Summary: "Learn how to recycle old clothes into brand-new fashions with these fun do-it-yourself activities"—Provided by publisher.
  Audience: Grade 4 to 6.
  Includes bibliographical references and index.
  ISBN 978-1-63188-871-7 (lib. bdg.)— ISBN 978-1-63188-883-0 (pbk.) — ISBN 978-1-63188-895-3 (pdf) — ISBN 978-1-63188-907-3 (e-book)
  1. Clothing and dress—Remaking—Juvenile literature. 2. T-shirts—Juvenile literature. 3. Decoration and ornament—Juvenile literature. 4. Fashion design—Juvenile literature. I. Title. II. Series: 21st century skills innovation library. Makers as innovators.
  TT550.F66 2015
  646.4—dc23
                                    2014035289

Cherry Lake Publishing would like to acknowledge the work of The Partnership for 21st Century Skills. Please visit www.p21.org for more information.

Printed in the United States of America
Corporate Graphics Inc.
January 2015

A fashion hacker might turn t-shirt sleeves into fingerless gloves.

give them a new purpose. Your parents might hack a kitchen table into a coffee table by shortening its legs. Your teacher might hack an old ironing board into a podium for class lectures by removing its fabric cover. Your neighbor might hack a vase into a lamp. In each of these cases, the hacker took something and transformed it into something else.

Hacking fashion is a great way to customize the things you wear. In this book, we'll look at one of the easiest things to find and hack: a t-shirt. T-shirts are great for beginning fashion hackers because they won't **fray** when you wash them. That means you don't have to **hem** the fabric. In this book, you'll learn how to paint, braid, knot, or fringe t-shirts into unique custom wearables.

To get started, you'll need a few supplies, including t-shirts! You can use brand-new shirts, but it's a lot more fun to work with something you already own (with your parents' permission, of course), a hand-me-down, or a thrift shop purchase.

All of the items in this book were made from secondhand t-shirts. They are cheap and already worn in, so they're nice and soft. You might want a few shirts in your own size, especially if you are just planning to paint the front. However, the real fun comes in buying over-sized t-shirts from the men's department. A bigger size means more fabric and more hacking possibilities.

As you shop, you'll notice that some t-shirts seem softer than others. The softest t-shirts tend to be made of a polyester-cotton blend. They're good for projects where the fabric doesn't need to be strong and it's okay if it stretches a lot. For example, if you cut the neck band off of a polyester-cotton-blend t-shirt, the neck might look droopy. That would be cool for some projects but not all. Stiffer shirts are probably made from 100 percent cotton. This material is sturdier, but it can look bulkier or boxier on your body. If you cut the neck band off of a 100 percent cotton t-shirt, the fabric will keep its shape. Try a few shirts of each kind and see what works best for your projects.

There's no one right way when it comes to fashion hacking.

Get at least four or five shirts to start with. If your first few creations don't turn out the way you expected, you can grab a new shirt and try again. Don't throw away your mistakes, though! Those scraps can easily be turned into pockets, flowers, headbands, and other pieces of future projects. Stash your mistakes in a shoe box for later.

Use your imagination to turn an old t-shirt into a brand new design.

Fashion Hacking Supplies

Must-Haves

A box in which to store your t-shirts and
   supplies

Lots of used long- and/or short-sleeved t-shirts

A sharp pair of scissors

Pins

Thread

Sharp hand-sewing needles

A clothes iron and ironing board

Craft or fabric paint

Stencil brushes or dish sponges

Paper towels

Freezer paper

Disposable plates

Chalk

Old newspaper

Optional Additions

A flexible tape measure made for sewing

A notebook or online account where you can sketch or paste ideas for projects

You might want to start a notebook or—with your parents' permission—an online clipping account such as Pinterest.com or Evernote.com, where you can save ideas for future projects. Once you get started customizing your wardrobe, you're in for a lifetime of made-for-you clothes, costumes, and accessories.

Chapter 2

Paint and Stencils

Every hacking project begins with examining an object for its possibilities. Here are two good questions to ask yourself as you examine shirts for your projects:

- Do I want to decorate this shirt but keep it mostly the way it looks now?
- Do I want to transform this shirt by altering its size or **silhouette**?

Gather your supplies before getting started on a project.

Pick Out Your Paint

In this chapter, we'll customize shirts using paint. Fabric paint works best. It's the most flexible when it dries, and it stays in great shape when you wash it. You can buy fabric paint for about $2.00 per tube at craft and fabric supply stores. It comes in many colors. Acrylic craft paint comes in even more colors and costs around $1.00 per tube. When acrylic paint dries on fabric, it will be stiffer than fabric paint.

Get Your Workspace Ready

You will need a protective covering to make sure you don't get paint on your work surface. Vinyl tablecloths work great for this purpose. So do camping tarps or cut-open garbage bags laid flat on your table or floor.

Put On Your Paint Clothes

Even if you are careful and your paint is washable, you should wear old clothes when you work. You don't want to ruin your favorite shirt while you create a new one! You should also roll up your sleeves so they don't drag and spread paint where you don't want it.

Start by laying your shirt out and figuring out where you want your design to go.

Prep Your Shirt

If you want your design to be centered on your shirt, you can make temporary marks to serve as a guide while you work. Fold the shirt in half lengthwise from the neck all the way down the center. Mark chalk along the fold, then unfold it. If you need another measurement mark, draw another line horizontally across the chest of your shirt. You can also eyeball it, which means to just make a good guess about where the design belongs.

You can even use the chalk to gently mark out the pattern you want to paint. If your fabric is thin and light-colored, try placing a drawing underneath and trace it onto the shirt. If you make a mistake, it's easy to rub off the chalk and try again. Paint mistakes don't rub off so easily. They will need to be painted over.

Grab a newspaper and carefully insert it between the layers of your shirt so you have a newspaper

Drying and Finishing Your Painted Garment

You can let your painted designs dry naturally in the air, but this can take some time. If you're in a hurry, use a hair dryer set to low heat and low speed to make your paint dry faster. Once it is dry, it is time to finish the design so the paint stays in place. Place a paper towel over the dry paint and go over it several times with a dry, no-steam iron to permanently set the paint in the fabric. Most custom-painted t-shirts should be washed in cold water and air-dried. However, there might be other steps to washing certain kinds of paint. Be sure to read the instructions on your paint bottle.

Place newspaper underneath the section of t-shirt you'll be painting. If you use a stencil or anything to help you draw a design, put that on top.

sandwich. The front of your shirt should be on top, then the newspaper, then the bottom of your shirt. Sometimes paint seeps through t-shirt fabric. If it does, the newspaper will protect the back of your shirt!

Don't squeeze out too much paint at once.

Paint!

Put a small squirt of paint about the size of a quarter on a paper, foam, or plastic plate. You can always add more, but you don't want a big bowlful of paint. (What if your cat suddenly jumps on the table and turns it over?)

Take a look at your brushes. Some of them come to a thin point at the end. These are good for fine lines. Some have a flat set of bristles. These are good when you want to create lines that can get fatter and thinner. Use a wider brush when you want to fill in a large space. You also have some cool brushes right on your hand. What happens if you dip your fingers or thumb into paint and make designs with them?

Dip your brush in the paint and gently wipe about half of it off. Practice your design on a scrap of fabric or a paper towel first. When you paint on fabric, use a little bit at a time and plan to paint several thin layers. Thin layers help you create clean lines and avoid blobs.

Stencil

If you don't want to paint your shirt by hand, you can stencil it! A stencil is a cutout of a design. Lay it on top of your fabric and add thin layers of paint to the cut-out area. Your design will appear when you lift the stencil!

You can make inexpensive stencils using freezer paper from the grocery store. One side is white paper, and the other is thin plastic. Find it in the store near the aluminum foil and plastic wrap for about $3.00 per box.

Lay the plastic side of the freezer paper face down on your workspace. On the white side, draw a stencil freehand or use a scrapbooking machine such as a Cricut or a Silhouette to cut the shape for you. When you make your first stencils, try shapes that don't have a lot of detail. Stars, moons, hearts, and lines are good beginning shapes.

You can use a cutting board and a craft knife to carefully cut out the shape. Ask a parent or adult for help. You can also gently poke a hole in the center of your shape and cut it out with a pair of scissors.

Once your stencil is ready, take it and your t-shirt to your ironing board. If you don't have an ironing board, ask an adult to cover your workspace in three or four towels and to heat up an iron. Be very careful not to let the hot iron touch your table!

Place the stencil on your shirt with the plastic facing downward. Will you put the stencil on the front? On the sleeve? Down along the hem? On the back? It's up to you! If you are going to place it on the center of your shirt, match it up with the chalk lines you made when you folded the shirt in half each way. Now your stencil will be perfectly centered!

With an adult's help, use the iron's no-steam heat setting to gently melt the freezer paper's plastic onto your shirt. It will melt just enough to temporarily glue your stencil in place. You don't want your stencil to move or your painted image will move, too!

Got it? Now let's stencil! Gently dab a stencil brush or a corner from a kitchen sponge into your paint. Then tap it a few times on a paper towel to get the excess paint off. Apply a little bit of paint at a time by tapping the brush/sponge up and down. It's okay to get paint on the freezer paper! Try not to brush sideways— this can stretch your t-shirt and loosen the freezer paper. Your design will become **distorted** as the shirt stretches. Add more paint to your brush as you need it. When you're done, wait about 20 minutes for the paint to begin drying. Then gently peel off the freezer paper.

You can also use stencils to create shadow designs. Once your t-shirt and stencil are dry, reapply the stencil in a slightly different position from where you placed it before. Use a new paint color. When you peel up the freezer paper, you'll see some of the original color peeking out from behind the new color—instant shadow!

Try switching paint colors as you stencil. If your stencil is a sunset, try applying yellow paint to the top third of the sun's circle. Change to orange for the middle third and red for the bottom. By overlapping each color just a bit, you'll create a cool multicolor look. You can add an antique or old-fashioned look to a design by gently applying a light dusting of dark brown or black paint around the edges of your stencil.

Masking Tape Designs

Do you like shirts with lots of lines and shapes? Lay out masking tape on your t-shirt. Press it down carefully so it sticks around all the edges. (Frog Tape brand sticks really well, but it is more expensive.) Apply paint on and around the masking tape. Just like using a stencil, you should press down with the brush instead of moving it side to side. Wait for about 20 minutes for the paint to dry. Then remove the masking tape to reveal your design!

Paint all the way onto the edges of your stencil to make sure the full design shows up on your shirt.

Chapter 3

Cut It Up

Now that you've made a project or two, you might be feeling more adventurous. Let's start looking at t-shirts as fabric that you can manipulate or change. In this chapter, we'll look at several ways you can customize your t-shirt without sewing a stitch.

Grace wants some new clothes to wear, so she's laid out a t-shirt to see what options she has. As she looks at it, she's not thinking, "There's a sleeve, and

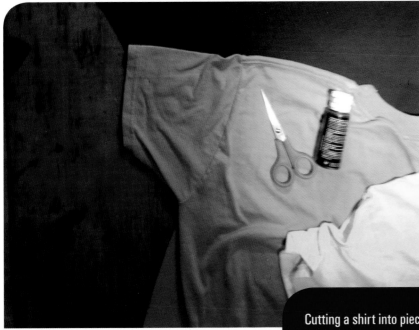

Cutting a shirt into pieces is a great way to get started on a hacking project.

there's the neckline." She's thinking about what she can do to turn the shirt into something completely different. Maybe that sleeve will become a cap or a bracelet. Maybe the neckline can be made into a headband or a flower pin. And if she cut off the bottom hem of a few t-shirts, she would have some instant belts . . . or an infinity scarf . . . or braids. Let's try it. Grab a sharp pair of scissors and a t-shirt you can cut up.

Shorten It!

Sometimes you have a cool t-shirt that's just too long. Try on the shirt. Ask a friend to help you mark a chalk line where you can cut it to be shorter. Use a ruler to measure the distance between the chalk line and the bottom hem. Mark that distance all the way around your

Convert Your T-Shirt into an Open-Front Cardigan

You can cut down the center of your t-shirt's front side to create a cardigan. This turns your pullover into an open-front creation. Start by folding your t-shirt down the middle from top to bottom. Use chalk to draw a line along the fold. Then cut along the chalk, starting at the neckline and going all the way down to the bottom hem. Only cut the front layer of the shirt! Now you can decorate the opening, tie it in a knot at your waist, trim it to a shorter length, or anything else you can think of!

shirt. Before you cut, put the shirt back on and raise your arms above your head. Ask your friend to let you know if the chalk line rises higher than you expected. If needed, adjust it before you cut. You can always cut off more if you need to, but you can't put the fabric back once it is gone.

Cut Off the Neckline

Carefully cut off the ribbing around the neck where the **seam** meets the t-shirt fabric. Try it on in different ways.

You can easily turn t-shirt pieces into a fun headband!

Can you wear it like a tennis pro around your forehead? Like a headband? What does it look like wrapped around your wrist? Could you cut it open to make a bookmark? Tie it around your backpack strap? Do you see all the possibilities that come just from one piece of the shirt? Be creative and try anything that comes to mind!

Cut Off the Sleeves

Take a long-sleeved shirt and, as you did with the neckline, find the seam where the sleeve meets the main part of the shirt. Carefully cut the sleeve side of the seam and not the shirt. It's easy to get another part of your shirt caught in your scissors!

Now you have kind of a funky round tube. Does it fit around your head? If so, you could tie a yarn knot around the top and make a hat. Could you trim it to make a mini pillow? What about turning part of it into a pocket for your new creation? Can you cut it into fringe? Could you fill a long sleeve and turn it into a weird stuffed animal with button eyes?

Chapter 4

Living on the Fringe

Fringe is a term that means loose threads or strips of fabric hanging from another piece of fabric. If you've ever seen a country singer wearing clothes with thin strips hanging off the sleeves, you've seen fringe. You can create fringe by cutting along the edge of a piece of t-shirt. For wide fringe, make cuts about 0.5 inches (1.3 centimeters) apart. For narrow fringe, try to leave about 0.25 inches (0.6 cm) between cuts.

Rock and Roll Bracelet

A fun way to start with fringe is to cut off a sleeve from a short-sleeved t-shirt following the directions in Chapter Three. Lay your sleeve down on a table. Now place your scissors along the edge that you cut from the shoulder. Cut a line into the sleeve that stops about 1 inch (2.5 cm) from the hem. Keep making fringe cuts until you have gone all the way around the sleeve.

Now you have fringe, but it looks flat. That's pretty interesting for some projects, but let's add some life. Gently tug each piece of fringe while holding onto the hem with your other hand. When you let go, your fringe should roll up, giving your project a unique look. Repeat this process for the remaining fringe strips. Now twist the sleeve around your wrist to make a cool bracelet!

Cut your fringe strips carefully, making sure that they are all the same width.

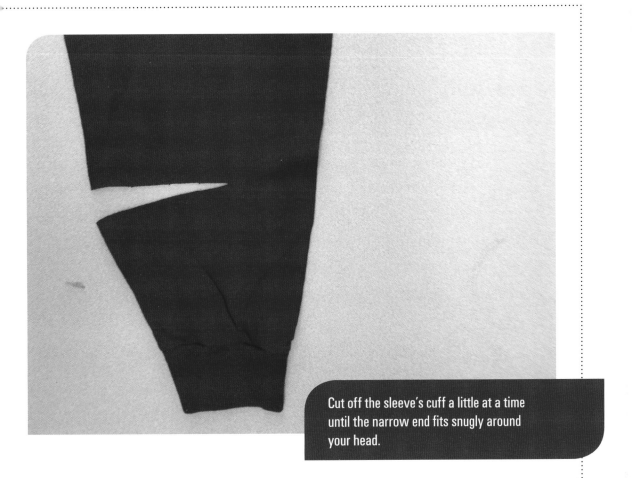

Cut off the sleeve's cuff a little at a time until the narrow end fits snugly around your head.

Crazy Hair

Cut off both sleeves on a long-sleeve t-shirt. Then cut off an inch or two of sleeve above the **cuff**. Does the sleeve stretch to fit around your head once the cuff is gone? If not, cut off another inch and keep trying until it does. Next, cut fringe lines from the shoulder until about 4 inches (10.2 cm) from the wrist end of the sleeve. You can try narrow 0.25-inch (0.6 cm) straight cuts like you did for the bracelet. You could also try crazy zigzag lines for an even weirder texture. Repeat the process for the second sleeve. Now put both sleeves on your head and enjoy your custom crazy hair! Mix up bright colors for a punk look. Mix gray, black, and purple sleeves to make a witch's wig.

No-Sew Tote Bag

You can turn a t-shirt into a handy bag that is perfect for shopping, going to the beach, or just about anything else. Cut off the neckline, sleeves, and bottom hem of a t-shirt. The t-shirt's sleeveless shoulders will serve as the bag's handles. Cut a fringe from the bottom of the shirt about 4 inches (10.2 cm) up. Tie one piece of fringe from the front of the shirt to another at the back of the shirt until all of the fringe has been knotted. Congratulations! You just made a tote bag! Experiment with longer or shorter fringe to test out your style. If you don't like the look of knots or fringe on the bottom of the bag, turn the t-shirt inside out before you make your knots. Turn it right side out when you're done tying knots to hide the fringe.

Chapter 5

Braiding Tricks

Another technique you can consider for your fashion hacking projects is braiding. Braiding is the process of weaving three strips of fabric together into a single ropelike piece.

Cut the hems off the bottoms of three adult-sized t-shirts. Tie all three strips of cloth into a knot at one end. Now lay them out on your table and spread out the three pieces. Each piece is called a strand. Gently pull the strand on the right toward the left. Lay it down

Braiding uses a lot of material, so start with longer pieces than you think you'll need!

between the other two strands. Now pull the piece on the left gently toward the right and set it down in the middle of the other two strands. Repeat this process over and over. Stop every few minutes to straighten out your braid and make it looser or tighter as needed. For a video demonstration, visit *www.youtube.com/watch?v=F_hHhtQGNus*. When you get to the end of your strands, see if your braid is long enough for the project you want to make. If not, sew, use fabric glue (let it dry before you continue braiding), or knot another length onto your strand and

Try weaving shirt strips into your hair to make a long, colorful braid.

Braiding Tricks

Here are some cool ideas for fashion hacks that use braids:

Hair Braids

Attach your finished braid onto a hair tie. Instant long hair!

Bracelet Braids

Tie both ends of your braid together to create a bracelet.

Belt Braids

Thread a braid through your belt loops and knot it for an instant custom belt. You can also tie your braided belt on top of a t-shirt or cardigan.

keep going. When you're done, tie all three strands into a knot at the loose end.

Throughout this book, you've seen many ideas for how to turn inexpensive leftover or secondhand t-shirts into new clothes and accessories. Hopefully by now you can take apart a t-shirt in your mind and imagine each part being cut, fringed, knotted, or braided into new ideas. Now go have fun. Get a pile of shirts and start making. You'll surprise yourself with what you can create!

Glossary

cuff (KUHF) the band or folded part of the sleeve of a shirt or blouse that goes around your wrist

distorted (dis-TORT-id) twisted out of a normal shape

fray (FRAY) to unravel

hem (HEM) to fold over and sew down an edge of material to prevent fraying

seam (SEEM) a line of sewing that joins two pieces of material

silhouette (sill-oo-ET) a dark outline of someone or something, visible against a light background

Find Out More

BOOKS

Chernin, Jan. *E-Textiles*. Ann Arbor, MI: Cherry Lake Publishing, 2013.

Kerr, Sophie, Weeks Ringle, and Bill Kerr. *A Kid's Guide to Sewing: 16 Fun Projects You'll Love to Make & Use.* Lafayette, CA: FunStitch Studio, 2013.

WEB SITES

Instructables
www.instructables.com
With a parent's permission, search this huge site of do-it-yourself projects for many more t-shirt hacks.

Pinterest
www.pinterest.com
With a parent's permission, search Pinterest for more t-shirt hacks.

Index

About the Author

Kristin Fontichiaro teaches at the University of Michigan. She loves to hack t-shirts with her niece, Grace, who created the hair braid and fingerless gloves projects for this book and helped to develop and test many others.